Inflation might almost be called legal counterfeiting.

—Irving Fisher, Economist
STABILIZING THE DOLLAR, 1920

The power of taxation by currency depreciation is one which has been inherent in the State since Rome discovered it.

—John Maynard Keynes, Economist
"Social Consequences of Changes
in the Value of Money"
in ESSAYS IN PERSUASION, 1933

About the Uncle Eric Series

The Uncle Eric series of books is written by Richard J. Maybury for young and old alike. Using the epistolary style of writing (using letters to tell a story), Mr. Maybury plays the part of an economist writing a series of letters to his niece or nephew. Using stories and examples, he gives interesting and clear explanations of topics that are generally thought to be too difficult for anyone but experts.

Mr. Maybury warns, "beware of anyone who tells you a topic is above you or better left to experts. Many people are twice as smart as they think they are, but they've been intimidated into believing some topics are above them. You can understand almost anything if it is explained well."

The series is called UNCLE ERIC'S MODEL OF HOW THE WORLD WORKS. In the series, Mr. Maybury writes from the political, legal, and economic viewpoint of America's Founders. The books can be read in any order and have been written to stand alone. To get the most from each one, however, Mr. Maybury suggests the following order of reading:

Uncle Eric's Model
of How the World Works

Uncle Eric Talks About Personal, Career, and Financial Security

Whatever Happened to Penny Candy?

Whatever Happened to Justice?

Are You Liberal? Conservative? or Confused?

Ancient Rome: How It Affects You Today

Evaluating Books: What Would Thomas Jefferson Think About This?

The Money Mystery

The Clipper Ship Strategy

The Thousand Year War in the Mideast

World War I: The Rest of the Story and How It Affects You Today

World War II: The Rest of the Story and How It Affects You Today

(Study guides available or forthcoming for above titles.)

An Uncle Eric Book

The Money Mystery

The hidden force affecting your career,
business, and investments

Third Edition

by Richard J. Maybury
(Uncle Eric)

First Sequel to
WHATEVER HAPPENED TO PENNY CANDY?

published by
Bluestocking Press
www.BluestockingPress.com

Printed and bound in the United States of America.
Cover illustration by Bob O'Hara, Georgetown, CA
Cover design by Brian C. Williams, El Dorado, CA
Edited by Jane A. Williams and Kathryn Daniels

Library of Congress Cataloging-in-Publication Data

Maybury, Rick.
  The money mystery : the hidden force affecting your career, business, and investments / by Richard J. Maybury.-- 3rd. ed.
      p. cm. -- (An "Uncle Eric" book)
  "First sequel to Whatever happened to penny candy?"
  Includes bibliographical references and index.
  ISBN-13: 978-0-942617-51-1 (soft cover : alk. paper)
  ISBN-10:   0-942617-51-7
  1. Money. 2. Monetary policy. 3. Financial security. I. Title
  II. Series: Maybury, Rick. "Uncle Eric" book.
  HG221.M125 2004
  332.4--dc21   2004007437

Published by Bluestocking Press • P.O. Box 1014
Placerville, CA 95667-1014
web site: www.BluestockingPress.com

To the center of my life,
Marilyn

> *"...the entire [Uncle Eric] series should be a required, integral, component of the social studies curriculum in all public and private schools. This would bring a quantum leap upward in the quality of citizenship in this country in a single generation."*
>
> —William P. Snavely
> Emeritus Professor of Economics
> George Mason University

Uncle Eric's Model of How the World Works

What is a model? In his book UNCLE ERIC TALKS ABOUT PERSONAL, CAREER, AND FINANCIAL SECURITY, Richard Maybury (Uncle Eric) explains that one of the most important things you can teach children or learn yourself is:

Models are how we think, they are how we understand how the world works. As we go through life we build these very complex pictures in our minds of how the world works, and we're constantly referring back to them—matching incoming data against our models. That's how we make sense of things.

One of the most important uses for models is in sorting incoming information to decide if it's important or not.

In most schools, models are never mentioned because the teachers are unaware of them. One of the most dangerous weaknesses in traditional education is that it contains no model for political history. Teachers teach what they were taught—and no one ever mentioned models to them, so they don't teach them to their students.

For the most part, children are just loaded down with collections of facts that they are made to memorize. Without good models, children have no way to know which facts are important and which are not. Students leave school thinking history is a senseless waste of time. Then, deprived of the real lessons of history, the student is vulnerable.

The question is, which models to teach. Mr. Maybury says, "The two models that I think are crucially important for everyone to learn are economics and law."

WHATEVER HAPPENED TO PENNY CANDY? explains the economic model, which is based on Austrian economics, the most free-market of all economic models. WHATEVER HAPPENED TO JUSTICE? explains the legal model and shows the connection between rational law and economic progress. The legal model is the old British common law—or Natural Law. The original principles on which America was founded were those of the old British common law.

These two books, PENNY CANDY and JUSTICE, provide the overall model of how human civilization works, especially the world of money.

Once the model is understood, read ARE YOU LIBERAL? CONSERVATIVE? OR CONFUSED? This book explains political philosophies relative to Uncle Eric's Model—and makes a strong case for consistency to that model, no exceptions.

Next, read ANCIENT ROME: HOW IT AFFECTS YOU TODAY, which shows what happens when a society ignores Uncle Eric's Model and embraces fascism—an all too common practice these days, although the word fascism is never used.

To help you locate books and authors generally in agreement with these economic and legal models, Mr. Maybury wrote EVALUATING BOOKS: WHAT WOULD THOMAS JEFFERSON THINK ABOUT THIS? This book provides guidelines for selecting books that are consistent with the principles of America's Founders. You can apply these guidelines to books, movies, news commentators, and current events—to any spoken or written medium.

Further expanding on the economic model, THE MONEY MYSTERY explains the hidden force affecting your career, business, and investments. Some economists refer to this force as velocity, others to money demand. Whichever term is used, it is one of the least understood forces affecting your life. Knowing about velocity and money demand not only gives you an understanding of history that few others have, it prepares you to understand and avoid pitfalls in your career, business, and investments. THE MONEY MYSTERY is the first sequel to WHATEVER HAPPENED TO PENNY CANDY? It provides essential background for getting the most from THE CLIPPER SHIP STRATEGY.

THE CLIPPER SHIP STRATEGY explains how government's interference in the economy affects business, careers, and investments. It's a practical nuts-and-bolts strategy for prospering in our turbulent economy. This book is the second sequel to WHATEVER HAPPENED TO PENNY CANDY? and should be read after THE MONEY MYSTERY.

THE THOUSAND YEAR WAR IN THE MIDEAST: HOW IT AFFECTS YOU TODAY explains how events on the other side of the world a thousand years ago can affect us more than events in our own hometowns today. In the last quarter of the 20th century, the Thousand Year War has been the cause of great shocks to the investment markets—the oil embargoes, the Iranian hostage crisis, the Iraq-Kuwait war, the Caucasus Wars over the Caspian Sea oil basin, and September 11, 2001—and it is likely to remain so for decades to come. Forewarned is forearmed. You must understand where this war is leading to manage your career, business, and investments.

The explosion of the battleship Maine in Havana Harbor in 1898 was the beginning of a chain reaction that eventually led to the destruction of the World Trade Center. In his two-part World War series Richard Maybury explains that an unbroken line leads directly from the Spanish-American War through World War I, World War II, the Korean and Vietnam Wars, the Iraq-Kuwait War, and the "War on Terror" that began September 11, 2001. Mr. Maybury explains the other side of the story, the side you are not likely to get anywhere else, in this two-part World War series: WORLD WAR I: THE REST OF THE STORY AND HOW IT AFFECTS YOU TODAY and WORLD WAR II: THE REST OF THE STORY AND HOW IT AFFECTS YOU TODAY.

Uncle Eric's Model
of How the World Works

These books can be read in any order and have been written to stand alone. But to get the most from each one, Mr. Maybury suggests the following order of reading:

Book 1.   UNCLE ERIC TALKS ABOUT PERSONAL, CAREER, AND FINANCIAL SECURITY.
Uncle Eric's Model introduced. Models (or paradigms) are how people think; they are how we understand our world. To achieve success in our careers, investments, and every other part of our lives, we need sound models. These help us recognize and use the information that is important and bypass that which is not. In this book, Mr. Maybury introduces the model he has found most useful. These are explained in WHATEVER HAPPENED TO PENNY CANDY? WHATEVER HAPPENED TO JUSTICE? and THE CLIPPER SHIP STRATEGY.
(Study Guide available.)

Book 2. WHATEVER HAPPENED TO PENNY CANDY? A FAST, CLEAR, AND FUN EXPLANATION OF THE ECONOMICS YOU NEED FOR SUCCESS IN YOUR CAREER, BUSINESS, AND INVESTMENTS. The economic model explained. The clearest and most interesting explanation of economics around. Learn about investment cycles, velocity, business cycles, recessions, inflation, money demand, and more. Contains "Beyond the Basics," which supplements the basic ideas and is included for readers who choose to tackle more challenging concepts. Recommended by former U.S. Treasury Secretary William Simon and many others. *(Study Guide available.)*

Book 3. WHATEVER HAPPENED TO JUSTICE? The legal model explained. Explores America's legal heritage. Shows what is wrong with our legal system (and economy) and how to fix it. Discusses the difference between higher law and man-made law and the connection between rational law and economic prosperity. Introduces the two laws: 1) do all you have agreed to do, and 2) do not encroach on other persons or their property. *(Study Guide available.)*

Book 4. ARE YOU LIBERAL? CONSERVATIVE? OR CONFUSED? Political labels. What do they mean? Liberal, conservative, left, right, democrat, republican, moderate, socialist, libertarian, communist — what are their economic policies, and what plans do their promoters have for your money? Clear, concise explanations. Facts and fallacies. *(Study Guide available.)*

Book 5. ANCIENT ROME: HOW IT AFFECTS YOU TODAY. This book explains what happens when a society ignores the model. Are we heading for fascism like ancient Rome? Mr. Maybury uses historical events to explain current events, including the wars in the former Soviet Empire, and the legal and economic problems of America today. With the turmoil in Russia and Russia's return to fascism, you must read this book to understand your future. History does repeat. *(Study Guide available.)*

Book 6. EVALUATING BOOKS: WHAT WOULD THOMAS JEFFERSON THINK ABOUT THIS? Most books, magazines, and news stories are slanted against the principles of America's Founders. Often the writers are not aware of it, they simply write as they were taught. Learn how to identify the bias so you can make informed reading, listening, and viewing choices.

Book 7. THE MONEY MYSTERY: THE HIDDEN FORCE AFFECTING YOUR CAREER, BUSINESS, AND INVESTMENTS. The first sequel to WHATEVER HAPPENED TO PENNY CANDY? Some economists refer to velocity, others to money demand. However it is seen, it is one of the least understood forces affecting our businesses, careers, and investments—it is the financial trigger. This book discusses precautions you should take and explains why Federal Reserve officials remain so afraid of inflation. THE MONEY MYSTERY prepares you to understand and avoid pitfalls in your career, business, and investments. *(Study Guide available.)*

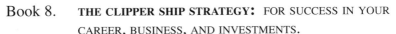
Book 8. **THE CLIPPER SHIP STRATEGY:** FOR SUCCESS IN YOUR
CAREER, BUSINESS, AND INVESTMENTS.
The second sequel to WHATEVER HAPPENED TO PENNY
CANDY? Conventional wisdom says that when the
government expands the money supply, the money
descends on the economy in a uniform blanket.
This is wrong. The money is injected into specific
locations causing hot spots or "cones" such as the
tech bubble of the 1990s. Mr. Maybury explains
his system for tracking and profiting from these
cones. Practical nuts-and-bolts strategy for
prospering in our turbulent economy.
(Study Guide available.)

Book 9. **THE THOUSAND YEAR WAR IN THE MIDEAST:** HOW IT
AFFECTS YOU TODAY.
Mr. Maybury shows that events on the other side
of the world a thousand years ago can affect us
more than events in our hometowns today. This
book explains the ten-century battle the U.S. has
entered against the Islamic world. It predicted the
events that began unfolding on September 11,
2001. It helps you understand the thinking of the
Muslims in the Mideast, and why the coming oil
war will affect investment markets around the
globe. In the last three decades this war has been
the cause of great shocks to the economy and
investment markets, including the oil embargoes,
the Iranian hostage crisis, the Iraq-Kuwait war,
the Caucasus Wars over the Caspian Sea oil basin,
and the September 11th attack—and it is likely to
remain so for decades to come. Forewarned is
forearmed. To successfully manage your career,

business, and investments, you must understand this war. *(Contact Bluestocking Press regarding Study Guide availability.)*

Book 10. WORLD WAR I: THE REST OF THE STORY AND HOW IT AFFECTS YOU TODAY, 1870 TO 1935.
The explosion of the battleship Maine in Havana Harbor in 1898 was the beginning of a chain reaction that continues today. Mr. Maybury presents an idea-based explanation of the First World War. He focuses on the ideas and events that led to World War I, events during the war, and how they led to World War II. Includes the ten deadly ideas that lead to war. *(Contact Bluestocking Press regarding Study Guide availability.)*

Book 11. WORLD WAR II: THE REST OF THE STORY AND HOW IT AFFECTS YOU TODAY, 1935 TO SEPTEMBER 11, 2001.
An idea-based explanation of the war. Focuses on events in the Second World War and how our misunderstanding of this war led to America's subsequent wars, including the Korean and Vietnam Wars, the Iraq-Kuwait War, and the "War on Terror" that began September 11, 2001. *(Contact Bluestocking Press regarding Study Guide availability.)*

Quantity Discounts Available

The Uncle Eric books are available at special quantity discounts for bulk purchases to individuals, businesses, schools, libraries, and associations.

For terms and discount schedule contact:

Special Sales Department
Bluestocking Press
Phone: 800-959-8586
email: CustomerService@BluestockingPress.com
web site: www.BluestockingPress.com

Specify how books are to be distributed: for classrooms, or as gifts, premiums, fund raisers—or to be resold.

Study Guide Available

A BLUESTOCKING GUIDE:
SOLVING THE MONEY MYSTERY

by Kathryn Daniels

based on Richard J. Maybury's book
THE MONEY MYSTERY

A BLUESTOCKING GUIDE: SOLVING THE MONEY MYSTERY is designed to enhance a student's understanding and retention of the subject matter presented in the corresponding primer: THE MONEY MYSTERY. This study guide includes comprehension questions and answers (relating to specific chapters within the primer), application questions (to guide the student in applying the concepts learned to everyday life), and a final exam. Also included are research and essay assignments, as well as thought questions to facilitate student-instructor discussion. In some cases, suggestions for further reading and/or viewing are listed.

Order from your favorite book store or direct from the publisher: Bluestocking Press (see order information on last page of this book).

Study Guides
are available or forthcoming
for other Uncle Eric books.

Contents

Note to Reader

Throughout the book, beginning with Chapter One, when a word that appears in the glossary is introduced in the text, it is displayed in **bold typeface.**

Author's Disclosure

For reasons I do not understand, writers today are supposed to be objective. Few disclose the viewpoints or opinions they use to decide what information is important and what is not, or what shall be presented or omitted.

I do not adhere to this standard and make no pretense of being objective. I am biased in favor of liberty, free markets, and international neutrality and proud of it. So I disclose my viewpoint, which you will find explained in detail in my other books.[1]

For those who have not yet read these publications, I call my viewpoint Juris Naturalism (pronounced *jur*-es *nach*-e-re-liz-em, sometimes abbreviated JN) meaning the belief in a natural law that is higher than any government's law. Here are six quotes from America's Founders that help to describe this viewpoint:

> ...all men are created equal, that they are endowed
> by their Creator with certain unalienable rights.
> —Declaration of Independence, 1776

> The natural rights of the colonists are these: first,
> a right to life; second to liberty; third to property; to-
> gether with the right to support and defend them in
> the best manner they can.
> —Samuel Adams, 1772

---

[1] See Richard Maybury's other Uncle Eric books, published by Bluestocking Press, web site: www.BluestockingPress.com, phone: 800-959-8586.

It is strangely absurd to suppose that a million of human beings collected together are not under the same moral laws which bind each of them separately.
—Thomas Jefferson, 1816

A wise and frugal government, which shall restrain men from injuring one another, which shall leave them otherwise free to regulate their own pursuits of industry and improvement, and shall not take from the mouth of labor the bread it has earned. This is the sum of good government.
—Thomas Jefferson, 1801

Not a place on earth might be so happy as America. Her situation is remote from all the wrangling world, and she has nothing to do but to trade with them.
—Thomas Paine, 1776

The great rule of conduct for us, in regard to foreign nations, is, in extending our commercial relations, to have with them as little political connection as possible.
—George Washington, 1796

George
Washington

Fable of the Frog

Once upon a time there was a frog who noticed his fellow frogs were being devoured by a snake. He fearfully went to a wise old owl and asked what to do. The owl said, "When the snake comes near, fly away." The frog thanked the owl for this sage advice and confidently hopped away.

A few days later the snake came. As the frog was disappearing down the snake's throat, he heard the owl say, "Sorry, I only deal with theory, not reality."

1

The Financial Panic of 1980

Dear Chris,

It was good hearing from you. I am not surprised that after studying the 1980s in your history class you are still confused about the economic events of that decade. Your observations are correct. For the most part history books report political history and ignore economic history. Without the economic side, historical events seldom make much sense. I am glad you wrote me, I'll try to help complete the picture for you.

You said you want to understand why economic times in the 1980s were so tough for so many people, including your parents and grandparents.

Your parents and grandparents have told me it's okay to discuss with you the roller coaster economic events that affected their lives. They all hope that after discussing these events with you, you'll be better prepared than they were to handle whatever comes your way.

To discuss the 1980s with a clear picture, however, we must go back at least to 1970, for the 1980s were the result of earlier events. We will look at the whole period from 1970 to 1990, as well as some events from the more distant past.

Chris, before we get started, you should review our prior correspondence about **economics.**[2] Pay particular attention to letters seven and eight to refresh your knowledge of **business cycles**, and the terms **money supply, velocity,** and **the demand for money.** It will only take a few minutes and will make what I am about to explain in my next few letters easier to understand since what's to come will be a continuation of our prior discussion.

I'll write again in a couple of days after you have had time to dig out those letters and review them. In my next letter, I'll talk about the government's manipulation of the economy, meaning its manipulation of your career, business, and investments. Then we will look at the financial panic of 1980 and the causes and ramifications of this panic.

I will finish this set of letters by discussing the short-term outlook you must adopt to cope with the new economic environment spawned by the 1980 panic.

Uncle Eric

---

[2] See WHATEVER HAPPENED TO PENNY CANDY? an Uncle Eric book by Richard Maybury, published by Bluestocking Press, web site: www.BluestockingPress.com, phone 800-959-8586.

2

A Shot of Inflation

Dear Chris,

Do you think the government manipulates our livelihoods as if we were puppets on a string?

Do you have any evidence to support your opinion?

Here are a few paragraphs from a news story that appeared in early 1986:

> In recent weeks the White House has made it clear that **Fed [Federal Reserve System]** Chairman Paul Volcker must march more to its tune in this critical congressional-election year...

> The President and some key advisers want Volcker poised to push easy **money** if the economy appears weak...

> Explains Washington insider Robert Strauss: "Volcker is a great chairman. Unfortunately, some areas of the country that want a shot of **inflation** will influence decision making this year. Volcker can't resist it."[3]

---

[3] "Economic Outlook," U.S. NEWS & WORLD REPORT, April 7, 1986, p. 64.

The use of monetary policy to "fine tune" the business cycle—meaning to fine tune our livelihoods and thereby influence elections—is an ancient art. Here is another news blurb from August 2, 1982:

> Before the Federal Reserve Board reduced its discount rate, at least two top White House aides bluntly told Chairman Paul Volcker that President Reagan wanted to see faster expansion of the money supply to cut interest rates and boost economic recovery before election day.[4]

This one appeared a few weeks later:

> Many suspicious Democrats in Congress openly predict that the drop in interest rates won't last. Their scenario: The Federal Reserve Board will permit borrowing costs to decline only until after the November 2nd elections—to take Reagan and the Republicans off the hook.[5]

The suspicious Democrats were right. Immediately after the 1982 elections, interest rates went into a two-year uptrend. This uptrend ended just before the 1984 elections.

As the two news blurbs show, business conditions are not manipulated for the benefit of the people, they are manipulated for the benefit of the government.

Does **political power** corrupt?

What do you think?

---

[4] Ibid., August 2, 1982, p. 16.
[5] Ibid., August 30, 1982, p. 11.

Ever since the creation of the Federal Reserve System in 1913, officials have been "adjusting" business conditions. Thousands of businesses, careers, and investments have been mangled and twisted as easily as coat hanger wires to fit the needs of each successive administration.

Officials thought they could do this forever, but they were wrong. By 1980, metal fatigue had set in and the wires were in danger of breaking. The panic of 1980 was a warning.

I will explain this warning shortly, but first I need to say a few words about the fact that government officials never discuss this warning; they are too busy generating misleading propaganda. It is this misleading propaganda that trapped your parents, grandparents, and a lot of other innocent people.

Uncle Eric

P.S. Chris, the reason I write these letters is to give you a viewpoint you won't get anywhere else. Few people talk about what's *really* happening when government officials change laws and policies. If you don't get this side of the story from me you will probably never get it at all.

3

Misleading Propaganda

Dear Chris,

Throughout most of the 1980s officials praised the economic recovery. Ecstatic that the 1982 recession had ended, they boasted about their astute handling of economic policy.

In 1983 and 1984 many employers assumed these official pronouncements about the recovery were true and they began expanding. Your dad was one of them. He invested heavily in a new office building, computers, and hired more workers. Employers bet heavily that the recovery was real.

The superstar of high tech, Apple® computer, launched its new Macintosh® line of personal computers. But sales of the new miracle PC did not achieve expectations, and in June 1985 Apple® announced the closing of three of its six plants and layoffs of 1,200 workers. Its stock fell to $14.62 from a January high of $30. This at a time when the so-called recovery was roaring.

By the end of the decade the truth about the recovery was widely known. The Reagan era boom had not been nationwide; it had been confined to certain areas, notably the stock market and the two coasts — much between the two coasts was still hurting.

Why was it confined to the stock market and the coasts? It has something to do with a process economists call the **injection effect**. It's too complex to explain in this set of letters, but I promise I'll cover it in a future set.[6] Our subject for now is the little known forces of velocity and the demand for money. To continue...

Houston and Denver were in **depressions**. U.S. car sales remained below the levels of the early 1970s.[7] The banking system was a mess — the rescue of the Savings & Loans would cost more than $100 billion. The oil industry was still distressed. Farmers were nowhere near as well off as they had been in the previous decade. The 1987 crash had decimated Wall Street's financial firms.

Perhaps the most important but least publicized story was the growing hardship of the young. The "real" (inflation-adjusted) average income of families headed by persons under age 30 (which included your parents) had plunged 14 percent.[8] Persons over age 40 were doing wonderfully, but poverty among the under-30 generation had nearly doubled.[9]

The American economy had been severely damaged at the start of the decade, before Mr. Reagan came to power, and by the end of the decade it was still damaged. There had been no real recovery.

---

[6] See THE CLIPPER SHIP STRATEGY, an Uncle Eric book by Richard Maybury, published by Bluestocking Press, phone: 800-959-8586, web site: www.BluestockingPress.com

[7] THE ECONOMIST, April 1, 1989, p. 62.

[8] "America's Income Gap, The Closer You Look, The Worse It Gets," BUSINESS WEEK, April 17, 1989, p. 78.

[9] Ibid.

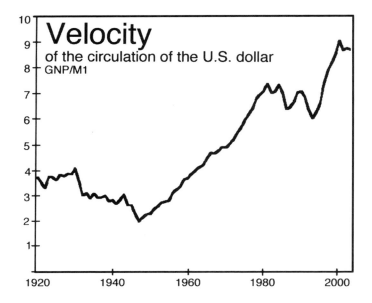

Velocity of Circulation of the U.S. Dollar

Velocity is the speed at which dollars change hands. It is a measure of the demand for money, which is the willingness of people to hold dollars.

When velocity is high, people are trading their dollars away quickly, which means the demand for dollars is low.

When velocity is low, people are trading their dollars away slowly, which means the demand for dollars is high.

Velocity was in a stable rising trend for 35 years after World War II. The financial panic of 1980 broke this trend, and velocity has remained unstable ever since.

This has left federal officials with a major problem. How do they know what the supply of dollars should be when they do not know what the demand for dollars will be?

What happened? We cannot be sure, economics is not an exact science, but studies show the velocity of circulation of the dollar had become erratic and gone into decline. Each time the Federal Reserve injected money into the economy to spark a recovery, the injection was offset by a fall in velocity—a repeat of the experience of the 1930s Great Depression.

The news media reported almost none of this because so few Americans knew enough economics to understand. In fact, I doubt many reporters or editors understood. (Most still don't.) But the Federal Reserve's economists discussed it incessantly in the Fed's publications.

For a small sample of these discussions read:

- "Money & Velocity in the 1980s" by John B. Carlson and John N. McElraveny, ECONOMIC COMMENTARY, Federal Reserve Bank of Cleveland, January 15, 1989.

- "Solving the 1980s' Velocity Puzzle: A Progress Report," by Courtenay C. Stone & Daniel L. Thornton, REVIEW, Federal Reserve Bank of St. Louis, August 1987.

- "Money Demand—Some Long Run Properties," QUARTERLY REVIEW, Federal Reserve Bank of New York, Spring 1988.

- "Monetarism and the M1 Target" by William T. Gavin, ECONOMIC COMMENTARY, Federal Reserve Bank of Cleveland, October 1, 1986.

These are complex, scholarly articles written for economists, but if you want to get into the subject deeply, you might try them. Unfortunately, I don't know of anything about velocity and the demand for money that's written on a level most people could understand. This is why I write you these letters.

You can see from the chart that after World War II, velocity went into a stable uptrend for 35 years. This stability ended in 1980 and, as far as we know, has never returned.

Clearly, something dramatic happened to velocity and the demand for money in the U.S. To understand it we need to learn a bit more about velocity and the financial panic of 1980. Then we will look at the great crash of 1987 and the meaning of all this for our future.

Uncle Eric

4

The French Example

Dear Chris,

To understand the velocity puzzle today it helps to study a historical parallel. True stories are easier to understand than mathematical models—and history is often repeated.

The following description of velocity in action during the great French **runaway inflation** is taken from Andrew Dickson White's fine book FIAT MONEY INFLATION IN FRANCE published and presented to members of the U.S. House and Senate in 1876.

In 1790 the French government was running short of cash and searching for a new way to finance its spending. Fearful of a tax rebellion, the politicians hit on a bold new plan to pay for everything they were buying. They began printing money.

This plan was popular; it enabled the French government to pay its debts and engage in all kinds of new activities without burdening the people with higher taxes.

The **paper money** was called the **assignat** (English pronunciation ass-ig-nat) and when it was first issued it was widely accepted. But this first stage of the inflation lasted only a few months. Each time a new wave of assignats was injected into the economy the value of each individual assignat fell. Prices rose to compensate for the assignat's fall in value.

In my previous set of letters[10] we covered the three stages of inflation. In the **first stage**, prices do not rise as fast as the money supply does because people don't know what is happening. Some delay their spending in hopes prices will fall back. In effect, they take some of the money out of circulation as the government is pumping it in. That was France in 1790.

In the **second stage**, many people have caught on and are spending their money quickly. Prices rise faster than the money supply because each unit of the money is changing hands faster. Many people want to get rid of it quickly and are willing to accept less for it.

In the **third stage**, the runaway, the whole population is in a panic to get rid of the money as soon as they get their hands on it, and the money declines to its real value, which is the value of scrap paper.

In 1790 France, the first stage of assignat inflation quickly gave way to the second stage as people began to get wise to what was happening. Knowing their paper money was losing value, they would not save it. Each time a person received an assignat, he would rush out and spend it before its value could fall further. Demand for the assignat weakened and velocity increased.

The merchants accepting the assignats knew the value of the money was falling and needed some way to protect themselves against the risks of accepting it. Some decided to

---

[10] See WHATEVER HAPPENED TO PENNY CANDY?, an Uncle Eric book by Richard Maybury, published by Bluestocking Press, phone 800-959-8586, web site: www.BluestockingPress.com

avoid the risk altogether by trading their goods or services only for gold or silver, which they knew the government could not create on a printing press.

Others continued accepting paper money but with a difference. Mr. White explained that in setting prices, "the merchant was forced to add to his ordinary profit a sum sufficient to cover probable or possible fluctuations in value."

To pay the higher prices demanded by its suppliers, the government printed more paper money. Like a dog chasing its tail, the inflation grew worse. The demand for money kept falling and velocity kept increasing.

By 1793, an item that cost 25 assignats in 1790 had risen to 1,000 assignats. A mere six months later it had risen to 7,000.

The demand for the assignat was falling like a rock as, in White's words, "everyone endeavors to invest his doubtful paper in buildings, machines, and goods, which, under all circumstances, retain some intrinsic value."

A full-blown stage three inflation was fast developing and the politicians were becoming desperate. To stop the decline in demand for the assignat they enacted wage and price controls. These controls forbade anyone to sell goods or services above certain stated prices. They also forbade any trade in gold, silver, or foreign currencies; the penalty for breaking these laws was a stiff fine.

So a **black market**[11] developed. People began spending their assignats covertly in order to get rid of them as fast as possible.

---

[11] A black market is the production, sale, or trade of goods or services against the wishes of the government.

The politicians decided the solution to this problem was to put more teeth into the law. The fine was increased. This had little effect, so even more teeth were added. Anyone caught trading with gold, silver, or foreign currencies was sentenced to six years in prison. A second offense was twenty years.

Still the black market flourished. Demand for the assignat continued falling and prices continued rising. Soap sellers in Paris had to add so much cushion into their prices to protect against the declining value of the paper money that washerwomen could hardly afford to purchase soap. In danger of losing their ability to earn their livings, mobs of angry washerwomen demanded that anyone who sold soap at high prices be punished with death. Yes, death. A runaway inflation can do terrible things to people. It can turn them into a mob.

On February 28, 1793, a riot swept Paris. Mobs of men and women went from bakery to bakery stealing bread—it was too expensive for them to buy. When the bread ran out, they began stealing rice and sugar and then anything else they could carry away.

The French politicians were becoming more desperate to stop the declining demand for assignats. In May 1793, they took the final step declaring the death penalty for any person convicted of "having asked, before a bargain was concluded, in what money payment was to be made."

To keep their desperate countrymen from fleeing the chaos, they also declared the death penalty for any Frenchman caught investing in a foreign country.

These brutal measures worked to some extent. The inflation cooled a bit, for a while; stage three was reduced to stage two. But the respite was only temporary and by 1795, the inflation was again solidly into stage three. Despite the price controls, a measure of flour that cost two assignats in 1790 was now at 225.

Debtors were ecstatic. Anyone who had borrowed 10,000 assignats in 1790 could repay the debt with the equivalent of 35 assignats.

Finally the desperate French politicians decided to scrap the assignat and replace it with a new currency, the **mandat**. But the mandat turned out to be an even worse failure than the assignat. The French people had learned their lesson about paper money, and demand for the mandat began to soften even before the new currency was off the presses.

For the mandat there was no stage one. As the new money entered the economy it entered already in stage two. The first mandats were accepted at only 35 percent of their face value. This quickly fell to 15 percent and, within six months, the mandat was in stage three — trading at only three percent of its face value.

The fines and imprisonment designed to prop up the demand for the assignat were revived for the mandat. Anyone who was overheard speaking as little as a single word against the mandat could be placed in irons for four years.

But nothing worked and velocity continued to soar. By May 1797, the demand for paper money had sunk to zero. No one would accept it in trade for anything; it was worthless.

Deprived of a reliable currency for conducting trade, the French economy was a shambles. Unemployment, fear, and hunger stalked the land.

Finally in 1799 there was a **coup d' etat** in which the government was overthrown and replaced by a strong, ruthless **dictator** — a man of action. He vowed that as long as he lived he would never again permit the French government to issue paper money. His name was Napoleon Bonaparte and his lust for political power threw Europe into one of the worst orgies of bloodshed ever known.

The French example demonstrates that when it comes to producing desperation, chaos, and war, few things work as well as paper money.

The point to remember is that there is nothing to keep any of this from happening again in the U.S. — in the whole world — at any time. In 1979-80 it nearly did.

> That paper money has some advantages, is admitted. But that its abuses also are inevitable, and, by breaking up the measure of value, makes a lottery of all private property, cannot be denied. Shall we ever be able to put a constitutional veto on it?

> — Thomas Jefferson, 1817

> Uncle Eric

5

Stage Two Inflation

Dear Chris,

In 1976, James Earl Carter was elected president largely on the assumption he would end the corruption that grew during the Nixon years.

The new Carter administration immediately began printing dollars to finance its spending.

During the first two years of Mr. Carter's reign, the number of dollars in the U.S. economy increased by 55 billion, or 18 percent. This rapid inflation of the money supply did not escape the notice of foreign holders of dollars, and these people began dumping their dollars in favor of assets that could not be created out of thin air—gold and silver.

At the time of Mr. Carter's election, gold was about $100 per ounce. A year later investors were getting nervous and gold hit $150 per ounce. A year after that they were even more nervous and gold hit $200 per ounce.

Mr. Carter's economic advisors said the demand for gold was nothing to worry about; expansion of the money supply could continue without danger. They said the "barbaric relic" (gold) was no longer important in world affairs.

Unfortunately, the application was not quite so neat as the theory. In 1979, the barbaric relic was at $300 per ounce and rising, and the nation was clearly in a stage two inflation. The Carter administration finally realized it had better do something to stop the declining demand for the dollar. Investors worldwide were becoming frightened. There was serious danger the inflation would slip into stage three and velocity would soar as it did in 1790s France.

As gold closed in on $400, Mr. Carter asked Paul Volcker to accept chairmanship of the Federal Reserve. Mr. Volcker did so, promising to restore confidence in the dollar.

October 6, 1979, brought an emergency meeting of the Federal Reserve Open Market Committee. The members unanimously agreed the Fed would no longer target interest rates; it would target money supply.

This meant the Fed would concentrate exclusively on keeping money supply growth within tightly defined boundaries allowing interest rates to go wherever this might send them.

This new monetary policy was enacted in concert with a Treasury announcement that Treasury gold would no longer be sold at regularly scheduled intervals. Fort Knox would be slowly drained at random times in random amounts. This, it was hoped, would throw a great deal of uncertainty into gold ownership and diminish the demand for gold.

The two actions had the desired effect. The demand for gold and silver stopped rising and the demand for the dollar appeared to be stabilizing—for a few weeks.

Uncle Eric

6

Khomeini

Dear Chris,

On November 3, 1979, followers of Ayatollah Khomeini seized the American embassy in Iran and took 52 hostages. They wanted the Shah.

In 1953, the U.S. Central Intelligence Agency had helped put the Shah, a ruthless dictator, in power. He became a long-time ally and Mideast surrogate of U.S. officials. His secret police brutalized thousands of innocent people. The Iranian militants wanted to give him (and the U.S. Government) a dose of his own medicine.

The Khomeini government could not or would not do anything about the hostages and neither could the Carter administration. With the 1980 election campaigns approaching, the politicians were desperate to do something to end the crisis quickly.

Someone came up with the "brilliant" idea of freezing[12] Iranian assets in the U.S. The theory behind the **freeze** was simple: You have our people and we have your money, let's deal.

---

[12] Freezing means holding in place. In effect, this was a confiscation of Iranian assets.

But the application was not quite so neat as the theory. The militants holding the hostages were not wealthy Iranians who kept their money in America, so they were quite immune to the freeze. They wanted the Shah and this is all they wanted; they couldn't have cared less if the freeze lasted forever.

So, the money stayed frozen.[13]   Mr. Carter could not release it because this would appear to the voters to be a capitulation. Week after week, with the world watching and waiting to see what would happen, both the money and the hostages remained imprisoned.

I should point out that a freeze is an extremely serious action normally taken only during a major war such as World War II. The reason is that millions of foreign investors keep their wealth in the form of dollars invested in America. They must not be frightened into dumping their dollars and fleeing America. If a freeze on one nation's assets occurs, they must be able to see quickly and clearly that the cause is so serious and unusual there is no danger of a freeze also happening to them.

But this was apparently not well understood by American officials. As the world watched and waited, other foreign investors began to wonder about the safety of their money. What might happen to my money, they asked, if my government does something to anger the American government? Will my money be frozen, too?

A **run** on the dollar began, first among wealthy Arabs whose governments were not on good terms with U.S. officials, then among wealthy persons worldwide. A panic

---

[13] In exchange for release of the hostages in 1981, U.S. officials gave back $3.89 billion but, at the end of the decade, some $5 billion remained frozen. Source: U.S. NEWS & WORLD REPORT, August 28, 1989, p. 89.

developed to convert dollars into gold and other currencies and move them beyond the grasp of the U.S. Government. Demand for the dollar plunged as the Fed's October 6th rescue package was overwhelmed. Gold headed for $600, and the disintegration of the world economy began to look like a serious possibility. The more knowledgeable investors began to remember the great French runaway inflation.

Unfortunately, few people in the news media understood such concepts as velocity and the demand for money, so most did not understand what they were watching. They reported it, but the reports were so scattered and disjointed you could understand only if you knew what to look for.

The November 26, 1979, U.S. NEWS & WORLD REPORT contained two important statements. First, "The dollar is faltering. Foreign holders of dollars are tempted to move to another currency fearing their funds in the U.S. could also be blocked." Second, "The U.S. decision has aroused concern over the fate of Arab assets and investments in case of mounting political differences between the Arabs and the U.S."

The December 17, 1979, BUSINESS WEEK reported, "The Iranian crisis and the freezing of Iranian assets have Europeans frightened about what will come next. 'The dollar is like a hot potato,' says Freidrich W. Menzel, managing director of Citibank in Frankfurt."

The Europeans' fears about the Carter administration's economic mistakes were soon fulfilled. Just when it appeared things could not get worse, they did. On December 24, Soviet troops marched into Afghanistan, and eleven days later the Carter administration levied the **grain embargo**.

Uncle Eric

7

The Grain Embargo

Dear Chris,

In retaliation for the invasion of Afghanistan, the Carter administration prohibited American farmers from selling grain to the **Soviet Union**.[14] Mr. Carter threatened additional grave consequences if the Soviet troops did not immediately withdraw.

The theory was that these pressures would cause the Soviets to leave Afghanistan and stability would be restored. But the application was not quite so neat as the theory.

The embargo and accompanying vague threats blew the lid off the currency markets. Around the world, people began to fear that U.S. officials would pressure their allies into freezing all **Soviet Bloc**[15] assets.

---

[14]   The Soviet government was a long-time enemy of the U.S. Government. The Soviet Union included the countries of Russia, Estonia, Latvia, Lithuania, Belarus, Ukraine, Moldova, Georgia, Armenia, Azerbaijan, Kazakhstan, Uzbekistan, Turkmenistan, Tajikistan, and Kirgizstan.

[15]   The Soviet Bloc was the Soviet Union plus the nations it controlled. This was a huge area, about one-sixth of all the land on earth.

At that time, Soviet Bloc debt to western banks totaled some $80 billion. Knowledgeable investors began to realize that if Soviet Bloc assets were frozen, the Soviet Bloc governments would be unable or unwilling to repay this debt.

With financial markets already in turmoil, an $80 billion default hitting dozens of large banks world-wide could set off a global bank run and financial crash every bit as bad as 1929.

Investors were also aware that each government would be tempted to try to bail out its banks by rapidly printing money and giving this money to the banks—by hyper-inflating.

All banks and currencies everywhere were now threatened by Mr. Carter's actions; no paper money of any type was trusted. The demand for all paper money plunged and the demand for gold and silver skyrocketed.

Gold During the 1979—'80 Panic

On January 31, 1980, THE WALL STREET JOURNAL quoted Hans Baer, chairman of Bank Julius Baer in Switzerland: "Put bluntly, the main reason for the gold-price explosion is the Iranian assets freeze. And after Afghanistan, people fear that there could be some joint assets freeze by NATO (North Atlantic Treaty Organization). This leaves only gold and silver. This panic carries a latent danger of a loss of confidence in the entire system."

Day after day the financial panic grew. The demand for paper money plunged. Gold rose to $850 and silver to $50.

But few people understood what was happening because few understood velocity or the demand for money. Most news people had their gaze fixed firmly on the supply of money, and since this supply was not increasing rapidly, they assumed the exploding gold and silver prices were an **anomaly**.[16]

The Fed did the only thing it could do. To offset the declining demand for the dollar, it tightened monetary policy stopping expansion of the money supply.

5-Year Treasury Security Rates

14%

10%

D J F M
1980

To restore confidence in the dollar and stop the panicky flight from dollars, the Federal Reserve restricted the money supply. This drove interest rates up three full points in one month.

---

[16] A strange exception to what would be expected.

Then it tightened further triggering a **deflation**. The tightening was reinforced by credit controls restricting the flow of money. Interest rates rose three full points in one month.

Officials held their breaths and waited. And waited. Finally the panic began to subside and precious metals prices broke downward.

After a few weeks had passed, investors lost their fear that the Carter administration would freeze Soviet Bloc assets. The perceived risk of holding bank deposits and paper money began to decline, and the demand for paper money began to stabilize. Interest rates fell back.

By May of 1980 the panic was over and paper money was again trusted—to some extent. As the LONDON TIMES wrote, investors in any given country now understand gold is an asset "no other government can inflate and no other government can block." And, as BUSINESS WEEK said, foreign bankers "will neither forgive nor forget" the panic of 1980.

Restoring confidence in the dollar would take a long, long time.

Uncle Eric

8

Ramifications of
the Panic of 1980

Dear Chris,

For several weeks in 1979-80 the world was approaching a financial catastrophe more massive than any seen before. Stage three inflation was developing *worldwide,* and there was danger all paper money would become worthless, destroyed not by skyrocketing supply but by plummeting demand.

But this catastrophe did not materialize, and the most important reason may be that we were lucky. Wealthy Arabs who had invested their money in America were as unsophisticated about velocity as almost everyone else. In 1979 much of their American holdings were in the form of **illiquid** long-term investments such as real estate.

These investments could not be dumped on a moment's notice the way bank accounts and other **liquid** investments could. So, no matter how frightened these Arab investors were in 1980, they could not bail out. This kept the crisis from being as bad as it could have been and eased the government's job of cooling the panic.

However, the wealthy Arabs learned much from the 1980 crisis. Writing in the March 23, 1984 edition of THE WALL STREET JOURNAL, reporter Michael Seist pointed out that these Arabs had changed the way they invest. "Many long-term investments, such as real estate and long-term government securities," Mr. Seist said, "are being turned into short-term investments like bank deposits." He also pointed out that, "Being highly liquid will make it that much easier for the Arabs to sell off their dollar portfolios" in the future.

Remember, this was *four years* after the panic. Wealthy foreign investors were still nervous and ready to bail out of dollars.

Uncle Eric

9

The Gloom-and-Doomers

Dear Chris,

Another of the fascinating aspects of the 1980 panic concerns the reactions of the so-called gloom-and-doomers. During the 1970s many financial experts had been acquiring the reputation for being gloom-and-doomers because they had been predicting a runaway inflation and economic catastrophe. Their predictions were based on the assumption money supply would skyrocket.

In 1980, money supply was not skyrocketing. It was increasing significantly but certainly not enough to cause a **hyperinflation**. Some gloom-and-doomers concluded that the soaring gold and silver prices were an anomaly unjustified by prevailing economic conditions.

Even today I occasionally see an article that mentions the "fact" that gold and silver prices of 1980 were simply "too high" or "at ridiculous levels." The writers are apparently assuming the demand for money is not an important factor. If money supply is not exploding upward, then there is nothing to cause the dollar to crash, they seem to believe.

But as we have seen, in 1980 the demand for money became more important than money supply, and I see no reason to assume this condition has changed.

Fed officials have quite a bit of control over money supply but almost none over the demand for money. The demand for money is a wild card; when it changes, all bets are off.

Uncle Eric

10

Two Important Questions

Dear Chris,

Perhaps the two most important questions to be asked about the panic of 1980 are: 1) how much did the politicians learn from their mistakes, and 2) how many of these politicians are still in the government today? The answers are, unfortunately, not much and not many.

The reason for the not much is simple. A politician does not get elected by understanding economics, finance, law, foreign affairs, or the other important subjects about which he makes daily decisions. He gets elected by understanding how to get elected. That's what a politician is—a person who is an expert at winning elections. Expecting politicians to make wise decisions about things they know little about is unrealistic to say the least.

It is hardly an accident that for eight years one of the most popular presidents of the most powerful government on earth was a professional actor.[17] Since the days of ancient Greece, politics has been show business—the art of illusion, and it has attracted the types of people who are specialists in this.

---

[17] Ronald Reagan.

So, once in power, few politicians are equipped to understand what they are doing with their power. This was painfully obvious in 1980.

It seems likely that many who participated in the 1979-80 mistakes that caused the demand for money to plummet and velocity to skyrocket are still quite hazy about what velocity and the demand for money really are. Before 1979 they probably did not even realize such forces existed.

But even if they did learn from their mistakes, few of them are still around, and those who are around have no intention of publicizing their mistakes. Today the Federal government is ruled by an entirely different set of politicians, most of whom are very likely as ignorant as their predecessors.

This was already clear in 1985 when President Reagan revealed he was considering freezing Nicaraguan assets. The mere fact that the president would *talk* about another freeze could have frightened enough foreign investors to trigger a plunge in the demand for dollars and a repeat of 1980. The panic didn't happen. Nicaragua was apparently seen by Arabs and other foreign investors as a special case unrelated to them—but the fact that Reagan was willing to take the risk tells us that little was learned from the 1980 debacle.

Indeed, it is quite possible that today's politicians not only did not learn crucial lessons from the 1980 crisis, they may have learned lessons that are wrong. They may understand so little about 1980, and about velocity and the demand for money, that they think Mr. Carter got away with it. So they may think they can, too. This is why it is important to be aware of what I call the financial hair-trigger, which I will introduce in the next letter.

Chris, I'd like to cite an example from the 1990s that demonstrates little was learned from the 1980 panic—the stock market. To end the 1982 recession, Federal Reserve officials injected tens of billions of dollars into the economy. To stop the 1987 crash and 1991 recession, they injected tens of billions more, and they did not stop.

By 1997, the market had become the largest bubble in the history of the world.[18] A feeding frenzy developed as thousands of investors who knew almost nothing about stocks or mutual funds bought and sold them like gambling addicts in a casino. The velocity of the money in the stock market is hard to measure with much accuracy, but any knowledgeable observer could see it must have been very high.

One way to measure velocity in the stock market is to look at the number of shares traded. Here are figures for the New York Stock Exchange.

Shares Traded on the New York Stock Exchange In Millions				
1980	1985	1990	1995	2000
11,562	27,774	39,946	87,873	262,477

Another way is to look at the value of the shares traded.

Value of Shares Traded on the New York Stock Exchange In Billions of Dollars				
1980	1985	1990	1995	2000
$382	$981	$1,336	$3,110	$11,060

---

[18] Largest in terms of the number of people and amount of money involved. A bubble is an economic hot spot created by the inflow of huge amounts of money. The stock market in the 1920s is the textbook example.

A completely accurate picture of velocity and the demand for money is never possible but, clearly, carloads of money were sloshing around in the stock market changing hands at a furious pace.

Uncle Eric

11

The Financial Hair-Trigger

Dear Chris,

In a free economy, change tends to be an evolutionary[19] process and you can plan ahead. In a government-controlled economy, change tends to be a revolutionary process[20] and you cannot plan ahead.

The evidence seems to show that velocity and the demand for money are not serious problems in a free economy. In the absence of **fiat**[21] **money** and **fiat law**, people have the ability to work, save, and invest without fear that the government will suddenly change the rules. Being able to plan ahead, they feel secure and are not inclined to panic. I know of no case in all of history when people panicked to bail out of cash when the cash was gold or silver.

But in a government-controlled economy like ours, many major changes are caused not by the masses of the people through gradual market mechanisms but by politicians and

---

[19] The word evolution here has nothing to do with Darwin. It means slow and gradual.

[20] Rapid, sudden.

[21] Something easily done or undone at the whim of authorities. Whimsical. Quantities of fiat money are easily changed.

bureaucrats in the centers of power. These politicians and bureaucrats are human and they change their minds. They occasionally cause massive, instantaneous reversals in economic trends. The 1979 freeze was only one of history's many electrifying examples. Another was the 1930 Smoot-Hawley tariffs that turned a recession into the Great Depression. In 1987, the Fed's tightening of monetary policy drove interest rates up and triggered a huge stock market crash.

The 1980 crisis was so widespread that wealthy individuals and organizations around the world learned unforgettable lessons about the insecurity inherent in a government-controlled economy. Like the wealthy Arabs in 1984, they are now much more uncomfortable being invested long-term.

This means a much larger portion of the money in the world is now what bankers call **hot money**. Its owners are quick to bail out if they catch the scent of trouble.

Thus the world financial system now has a financial hair-trigger. Millions of people are constantly alert and very sensitive to the slightest hint of change in government policy.

In other words, today any long-term plan is extremely risky. At any time, some politician or bureaucrat could utter an off-hand remark or casually suggest a strange new policy. This could scare enough people to pull the hair-trigger and start the stampede. You could be caught unprepared, as the Arabs were in 1980, helplessly watching the security and value of your business and investments—your whole way of life—rapidly undermined.

This is what happened to your parents. Your father's real estate business flourished in the 1970s when interest rates were low. People could easily borrow the money to buy homes and other types of real estate.

Then U.S. officials froze Iranian assets starting the great panic; the Soviet invasion of Afghanistan poured gasoline on the fire.

The only way the Federal Reserve could stop the panic was by restricting the money supply to offset the decline in the demand for money. This pushed **interest** rates[22] very high and triggered the back-to-back 1980 and 1982 recessions. Your father's business was destroyed by events on the other side of the world. Like most Americans, your parents didn't even know where Iran or Afghanistan were and never heard of the Shah. I know this is hard to believe in light of current events, but, at that time, few Americans could have pointed to Iran or Afghanistan on a map.

At that time, not unlike today, most teachers and textbooks failed to explain how events on the other side of the world could affect your parents in their own home town. So your parents, like most Americans, had a tunnel-vision view of the economy. They looked no further than their own country. Some looked no further than their own home town.

An example of how quickly panic can be generated and the demand for money can plunge in a government-controlled economy appeared in Argentina in the summer of 1985. When *rumors* began circulating that Argentine politicians were *thinking* of freezing prices and issuing a new currency, merchants jacked up prices overnight, some by 75 percent or more. Shoppers roared through the supermarkets sweeping goods from the shelves, and in two days of frantic black-market trading, the peso plunged 50 percent. On rumors!

---

[22] Interest is the price of renting money. When the supply of money is restricted, the price rises.

The moral of the story is: In a government-controlled economy, short-term plans are the only kind that involve reasonable risks. They enable you to shift gears quickly if trouble begins to develop. Long-term plans are invitations to financial suicide.

The great crash of 1987 was an object lesson about the financial hair-trigger. When the stock market began to plunge, the panic spread world-wide within hours. A deflationary catastrophe like the 1930s Great Depression was averted only by the Federal Reserve's solemn promise to inject however much money into the banking system as was necessary to stop the crash.

At the end of the decade the world's central bankers remained fearful; the lessons of the 1980 panic and 1987 crash had not been forgotten:

> In the late 1970s the Carter administration and the IMF [International Monetary Fund] sold over 3,000 tons of gold in an attempt to wean central bankers off the metal... But old habits die hard. The inflationary surge of 1979-81 made central bankers seek refuge in the traditional haven of gold. Even though inflation and gold prices have since fallen, the buying goes on. In seven of the past nine years central banks have been net buyers of gold, adding 983 tons to their holdings.
>
> —THE ECONOMIST, 8/19/89, p. 61

Uncle Eric

12

Federal Reserve Behavior

Dear Chris,

Some years ago, in testimony before Congress, Federal Reserve Chairman Paul Volcker was asked what the Fed was going to do next. Mr. Volcker admitted, "I don't know what the Federal Reserve is going to do next."[23]

The Fed has a serious problem; it does not know how to conduct monetary policy. How could it? There is no reasonable way to decide what to do with the supply of money when we do not know what the demand for money will be.

The demand for money is very difficult to measure with much accuracy, and it is impossible to **forecast** with much accuracy. Velocity calculations are of only slight help because they are so rough. The most commonly used measure is to divide **Gross National Product (GNP)** by the money supply to determine how many times the average dollar changed hands to make the production possible. In recent years this has run about nine times according to the (unreliable) statistics.

---

[23] WALL STREET JOURNAL, March 19, 1985.

But, in any given month or quarter, the calculations typically show wild swings of as much as plus or minus five percent—sometimes more.

If these calculations were accurate, they would be terrifying. A five percent increase in velocity is the equivalent of a five percent increase in the money supply—in one month!

The velocity calculations are useful only over very long time spans. When they are averaged over five or ten years they show rather distinct trends. But anyone who promises greater precision than this has either discovered an amazing new technique of measurement or is selling snake oil.

Velocity Statistics Are Erratic

Velocity statistics swing wildly from quarter to quarter. The years 1965-67 and 1983-84 were typical. A reasonably clear picture emerges only when the statistics are averaged over many years.

Other measures are sometimes used, for instance, the number of checks passing through the banks—but nothing has been found that is very accurate. Each individual makes daily buy and sell decisions depending on how he or she feels about the need for cash versus the need for goods or services. Tracking the attitudes of millions of people is simply impossible and will probably remain so forever. We all have free wills and change our minds frequently.

So, the Fed must decide what the money supply will be without having the slightest idea what the demand for money will be. Throughout 1984, for instance, velocity was rising (see the chart on the previous page). In the fourth quarter it registered a near four percent annual rate of increase. Then, in the first quarter of 1985, it made a complete reversal, falling at a four percent rate. If you were the Fed, what would you have done, tighten to offset the established rising trend or loosen to offset the new falling trend?

In making your decision you would have had to keep four points in mind.

First, you probably cannot know what velocity will be doing at the time you will be inflating or deflating. This can be seen by the fact that the 1980 crisis was so short-lived it has never shown up in the velocity statistics even though bankers and precious metals dealers worldwide were watching it happen all around them. Talk with some who are old enough to remember, and you will hear that on every continent investors were in a panic to get rid of their paper currencies and get into precious metals. The Federal Reserve was having historic emergency meetings to begin the tight money measures to combat the crisis, and the statistics never have shown the crisis even happened.

Second, if you inflated the money supply at, say, a 15 percent rate, at a time when velocity was rising at, say, 15 percent, then you would actually have been "pumping the accelerator" at 30 percent. *Without realizing it,* you would be flirting with another monetary disaster because 30 percent would certainly trigger a flight from the dollar if it continued very long.

Third, it is much easier to stop a deflation than an inflation. You can always print a few tons of money and pass it around to stop a deflation, but once inflation is into stage three your hands are tied and catastrophe is all but certain.

Fourth, recessions usually bring a cooling of velocity. They create a climate of fear that causes people to hoard cash.

So, you are a navigator without charts or compass. What do you do?

My guess is you would err on the side of caution. You would stay tight enough to keep the economy in a perpetual recession so that you could be sure you were not inflating too heavily. Staying in a recession would be the only way you could be confident you were not about to pull the financial hair-trigger and launch a hyperinflation.

In short, a recession would be your only reliable indicator that velocity was under control.

So, I believe this is why the 1980s recovery was a myth and why unemployment, poverty, and bankruptcies remained widespread for years. Federal officials had no choice but to keep the money supply tight and the economy in a recession until they were certain they had restored confidence in the dollar. My guess is it took ten years to do that, and your family was one of the victims.

In 1997, U.S. officials came out with a new way to track velocity and the demand for money. They now offer an "inflation-indexed" [24] **bond**. These new bonds pay interest that is tied to the **consumer price index** (CPI). When the CPI rises, the bond's interest rises, too.

The government's other bonds do not have this feature; their rates of interest are fixed. So when investors are getting nervous about the value of the dollar, the other bonds will not be as appealing as the new indexed bonds.

Officials will track the difference in demand between other bonds and indexed bonds. When they see the other bonds losing favor to the indexed bonds, they'll know investors are getting worried about the stability of the dollar.

Chris, I suggest you track the bonds yourself. THE WALL STREET JOURNAL and other financial publications report on them. A sharp increase in demand for "inflation-indexed" bonds over other bonds can be taken as an indicator that the demand for money is falling and velocity rising. The Fed will need to tighten the money supply and raise interest rates to restore confidence in the dollar. This will almost certainly mean a recession, or at least a slowdown, and a deflation of whatever hot spots exist at the time. If you are in one of these hot spots, this will be crucial information for you.

Mark this page, Chris, and refer back to it after you have finished reading my future set of letters about hot spots.[25] These new bonds will be very important to you.

Uncle Eric

---

[24] An IOU.

[25] Uncle Eric is referring to THE CLIPPER SHIP STRATEGY by Richard J. Maybury, published by Bluestocking Press, phone: 800-959-8586, web site: www.BluestockingPress.com

13

Another Important Lesson

Dear Chris,

From the Iranian assets freeze we learn another important lesson: have an international outlook. What the U.S. Government does on the other side of the world often affects you and your family more than what it does in your home town.

In fact, the government's foreign policy can completely overwhelm events at home. Aside from the panic of 1980, we also have the example of the Vietnam War. To finance it, the government created tens of billions of dollars and plunged us into the inflationary chaos of the 1970s.

The 1973 Arab-Israeli War is a further example. The U.S. Government's support of the Israeli government angered the Arab oil producers. The result was the Arab oil embargo, soaring oil prices, the "energy crisis," and the bankruptcies of thousands of firms.

The 1990 Iraqi invasion of Kuwait caused another crisis. The oil price doubled to $40 per barrel and the stock market dropped 19 percent.

In short, the world has been unified economically. Our transportation and communication systems are now so effective that all humankind lives in a single global economy.

But the governments do not like this; they fight it. They greedily cling to their borders, tariffs, and other artificial boundaries that should have vanished with the coming of the telephone and radio. This primitive behavior creates great risk for business people and investors as governments continue to fight over territory.[26]

Chris, a good research project is to go back through history and find more examples of events abroad affecting Americans at home. Americans do not have a tradition of watching events in foreign nations so they are often **blindsided**.[27] This creates an advantage for investors who do watch international events.

Uncle Eric

---

[26] This should not be taken as an endorsement for one world government. Far from it. It is simply the recognition that the world has already been unified economically and governments don't like it.

[27] A football term meaning to be hit from one direction while looking in the other direction.

14

The Lesson of the 1987 Crash

Dear Chris,

Years after the 1987 stock market crash we are still debating what it all means. I have two thoughts about it.

The first is simply that the crash was proof the hair-trigger existed at that time. By the mid-1990s, however, there was apparently some restoration of confidence as millions plunged into the stock market bubble. By 2002 that confidence had been severely shaken (again) by the stock market tech crash and 9-11.[28] I doubt there is much chance of the hair-trigger going away until the war ends, which could be decades.

The second thought is a bit more complex. The conventional view of the government's monetary policy is that officials try to inflate the money supply at a rate that will keep us in a safe zone between inflationary boom and deflationary bust. If they print too little money, we get a recession and, if they print too much, we get a **double-digit inflation**.

---

[28] On September 11, 2001, in an attack against the United States, over 3,000 civilians were murdered. The World Trade Center in New York was destroyed as well as a portion of the Pentagon. Four civilian airliners were destroyed, including passengers and crew. This attack is also referred to as Sept. 11, Sept. 11 Attack, and 9-11.

CONVENTIONAL VIEW
Federal Reserve Monetary Policy

The widespread assumption is that the Federal Reserve attempts to keep its monetary policy (rate of inflation of the money supply) running in a safe zone between parallel areas of boom and bust.

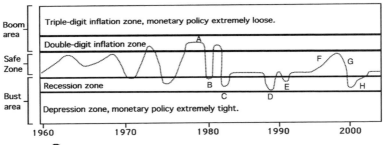

Federal Reserve monetary policy
A   Heavy inflation in late 1970s.
B   Mild recession in 1980. Inflation did not stop.
C   1982 recession was worst since Great Depression. Inflation reduced.
D   1987 stock crash, very severe.
E   1991 recession, mild. Inflation reduced.
F   Fed inflates stock market tech bubble.
G   Fed deflates stock market tech bubble. Worst stock crash since Great Depression.
H   2001 recession, mild.

This assumption that the lines are parallel is based on lack of understanding of the causes of business cycles. As explained in my seventh letter on economics,[29] when officials inject money into the economy, this causes business people to make mistakes. Firms are created and expanded and employees are hired in areas where they would not otherwise be — meaning in areas where the new money is appearing — and these firms and employees are then dependent on a continued flow of this money. If officials stop expanding the money supply, these firms and employees go broke. This disorganization of firms and employees is called the "injection effect."

Chris, I'll discuss the injection effect in a later set of letters.[30] It is crucially important for you to understand. If your parents had understood it in the 1980s, they would have stood a better chance of weathering the storm. They do understand now and plan all their business and investment decisions based on what I call the Clipper Ship Strategy.

Each injection of new money causes more disorganization of firms and employees, which means *the effects are cumulative.* Every year more people become dependent on the continued flow of newly printed money. In 1950, an injection of $10 billion stopped the recession; in 1983, $100 billion was needed; in 1993, $350 billion. An unknown but certainly large portion of that $350 billion ended up sloshing around in the stock market.

---

[29] See chapter seven, "Wallpaper, Wheelbarrows and Recessions" in WHATEVER HAPPENED TO PENNY CANDY? by Richard J. Maybury, published by Bluestocking Press, web site: www.BluestockingPress.com, phone: 800-959-8586.

[30] Uncle Eric is referring to Richard J. Maybury's book in THE CLIPPER SHIP STRATEGY, published by Bluestocking Press, web site: www.BluestockingPress.com, phone: 800-959-8586.

Because each injection causes more disorganization, the economy becomes more fragile. This is the lesson of the 1980 panic, the 1982 recession, the 1987 stock market crash, and the stock crash of the 1990s, which wiped out more wealth than any other stock crash in history. We are living in a crystal vase that cracks easily and may shatter. The vase is beautiful but delicate. The 1987 tightening of monetary policy was not at all severe, but it brought the worst stock market crash since 1929. The tightening at the end of the 1990s was similarly gentle, but it brought a crash that was, by many measures, the worst ever.

Combine all this disorganization of firms and employees with the financial-hair trigger that could cause velocity to soar and we get this picture of monetary policy.

MORE REALISTIC VIEW
Federal Reserve Monetary Policy

The lines between boom and bust are not parallel, they converge. The safe zone is narrowing because each injection of new money causes more disorganization of businesses; the economy is becoming more fragile.

The illustration is a theoretical model, not a forecast. It is meant only to give you a mental picture of what is happening. I do not know if the decade that began in 2000 will be when our luck will run out. Maybe we will make it into the next decade, maybe not. We might even make it to 2020 or 2030 without a major catastrophe; there is simply no way to know. Neither the extent of the disorganization nor the Fed's behavior are measurable or predictable.

I do not want to give the impression I am certain this view is correct. There isn't much in economics that we can be certain about; it's a young science. I am only saying that this picture seems to me to agree with the evidence better than the conventional picture does.

I am sure that we've seen this model at work in France, Argentina, Brazil, Mexico, Germany, and many other nations. Each injection of new money caused more disorganization and more fragility until officials finally went a bit too far in one direction or the other and triggered a runaway inflation or depression.

Chris, another research project for you would be to check into the runaway inflations and subsequent depressions that hit those countries. History does repeat.

You will find these economic crises almost always bring political upheaval. One of the most dramatic and well documented cases in history was Russia in the 1990s. I suggest you research that one first; it's so typical you can take it as a model for the others.

In fact, after you research 1990s Russia, go back and research the great panic of 1979-80, especially the emergency meetings at the Federal Reserve. By knowing what happened in Russia you will be able to see what federal officials were trying to avert in 1979-80.

Uncle Eric

15

What You Can Do About It

Dear Chris,

In planning your business and investment future, keep the following in mind: We cannot know what will happen next, so make plans accordingly. Keep all your time horizons short. *Don't get into anything you can't get out of fast.*

For your investments, do what central bankers do, own some gold and silver. Ten percent of your liquid assets in gold and silver coins is good insurance.

I believe these inflation hedges will stay down and perhaps even decline, or at least I hope so, as long as the dollar remains trusted. But sooner or later officials will make another mistake that will cause the demand for money to fall and velocity to soar, and when this happens we may not be as lucky as in 1980. This time the panic may not stop. If it doesn't, I would expect the precious metals to triple or quadruple within weeks.

U.S. Government Treasury Bills are an excellent protection against deflation. I always have a lot of those, but they require a minimum investment of $2,500 (via a Treasury Bill money market mutual fund). Until you accumulate that much savings, I suggest you put your money in U.S. Savings Bonds that you can get for as little as $25.00. Savings Bonds are equally good protection against deflation.

In your career or business be flexible and ready to make changes at any moment. I will explain that in great detail in a future set of letters.[31]

We saw a lot of history unfold during the 1980s and this was only the beginning. We will encounter many dangers and many opportunities; be ready for anything and spread the word.

Uncle Eric

---

[31] Uncle Eric is referring to Richard J. Maybury's book THE CLIPPER SHIP STRATEGY, published by Bluestocking Press, phone 800-959-8586, web site: www.BluestockingPress.com

Early Warning Symptoms

U.S. Treasury Secretary William Simon gave this testimony before the House Sub-Committee on Democratic Research Organization on April 30, 1976, just three years before the panic of 1979-80 began:

"In the case of the federal government, we can print money to pay for our folly for a time. But we will just continue to debase our currency, and then we will have financial collapse. This is the road we are on today. This is the direction in which the 'humanitarians' are leading us. But there is nothing 'humanitarian' about the collapse of a great industrial civilization. There is nothing 'humanitarian' about the panic, the chaos, the riots, the starvation, the death that will ensue. There is nothing 'humanitarian' about the dictatorship that must inevitably take over as terrified people cry out for leadership. There is nothing 'humanitarian' about the loss of freedom. That is why we must be concerned about the cancerous growth of government and its steady devouring of our citizens' productive energy. That is why we must be concerned about deficits and balancing the budget. The issue is not bookkeeping, it is not accounting. The issue is the liberty of the American people.

Forgive me, Mr. Chairman. I have not been addressing your specific questions. I just wanted to put the real issue in focus. I can speak to the technicalities, and I will do so. But they obscure the real issue that faces us in the country today. The problems of deficits, budget balancing, capital markets—all these are important. But it is more important, I think, to understand that these are just early warning symptoms of a disease that threatens the very life of our body politic. And if we continue to move down this same path, that disease will become irreversible, and our liberty will be lost. I speak of this so insistently because I hear no one discussing this danger. Congress does not discuss it. The press does not discuss it. Look around us— the press isn't even here! The people do not discuss it—they are unaware of it. No counterforce in America is being mobilized to fight this danger. The battle is being lost, and not a shot is being fired.

That, Mr. Chairman, is why for me the last few years in office have been like a bad dream. I am leaving Washington next January. I am going to go home to New Jersey a very frightened man."

—Treasury Secretary William Simon
April 30, 1976

When Mr. Simon gave this testimony, the U.S. money supply[32] was $300 billion. Within four years it was $400 billion and today it is $1.3 trillion.

In 1980, we dodged a bullet. Will we be this lucky the next time?

---

[32] Measured by M1.

16

Summary

Dear Chris,

Here is a summary of the important points covered in this set of letters:

1. The economy is not a machine; it is people. When the government makes "adjustments" to the economy it is manipulating the businesses, careers, and investments of innocent people.

2. Velocity and the demand for money are poorly understood and rarely discussed, but they are crucially important to us all.

3. History repeats. The French runaway inflation of the 1790s is filled with lessons for us today. Review the three stages of inflation so that you remember them well.

4. Economics is a young and very inexact science so we cannot be sure about very much. But it appears that

the great financial panic of 1980 was driven by rising velocity and the falling demand for money, not rising money supply.

5. The panic of 1980 was a demonstration of the fact that events in foreign countries can affect us more than events in our home towns. We should pay at least as much attention to the rest of the world as we do to our own country. (In a future set of letters I will help you get started by writing about the thousand year war in the Middle East and how it affects us today.[33])

6. In a free economy, change tends to be evolutionary. In a government-controlled economy, change tends to be revolutionary.

7. Velocity and the demand for money are extremely difficult to track. The new "inflation-indexed" bonds will be a big help.

8. For your investments, your long-term plan should be to have no long-term plan. We do not know what government officials will do, so don't get into anything you can't get out of fast, in a few days.

Chris, don't let the government's control over your future business, career, and investments get you down. There is a lot of truth to those old clichés: knowledge is power, and forewarned is forearmed.

---

[33] See THE THOUSAND YEAR WAR IN THE MIDEAST: HOW IT AFFECTS YOU TODAY by Richard Maybury, published by Bluestocking Press, phone 800-959-8586, web site: www.BluestockingPress.com

Having read this and my previous sets of letters, you know a great deal more about economics than most adults do, and you have a much better chance of protecting yourself and prospering. It's a great head start. A future set of letters will give you lots of specific nuts-and-bolts how-to advice.[34]

Until then make it a habit to learn everything you can about business, economics, and history, and encourage everyone you care about to do the same. It's not only fascinating, it is essential for achieving financial security.

Uncle Eric

Spread the Word!

---

[34] See THE CLIPPER SHIP STRATEGY, an Uncle Eric book by Richard Maybury, published by Bluestocking Press, phone 800-959-8586, web site: www.BluestockingPress.com

17

The Velocity Demon Updated
April 1999

*This chapter was added in the 1999 edition of THE MONEY MYSTERY.
I am leaving it exactly as it was written because its forecasts
turned out correct. Chapter 18 has been added as an update.*

—Richard J. Maybury (Uncle Eric)

Dear Chris,

It's been two years since I last wrote you in depth about
the subject of velocity. Much has happened, is happening, in
the world today and I think it's time to update you on the
subject.

As we approach the new millennium, the big war has not
started, although it certainly seems to be building; the economic turmoil is definitely here. Frequent articles are now
written about deflation and a possible depression.

Central bankers are attempting to inflate the depression
away by printing new money. In the final quarter of 1998, 37
central banks around the world made a total of 75 interest rate
cuts.[35] As I write this letter to you, Chris, it's spring 1999. In

---

35 THE WALL STREET JOURNAL, February 22, 1999, p.1.

the U.S. the money supply has been increasing at a 17% rate since summer 1998.

Yet, the worldwide deflation seems to be accelerating and fears of depression grow. In real terms THE ECONOMIST magazine index of raw materials prices is at its lowest in 150 years.[36]

What's happening?

I think it's velocity. We are repeating the 1930s experience. At that time central bankers inflated in an attempt to stop the Great Depression. Their attempts failed.

Between 1930 and 1940, the U.S. money supply was increased 54%; Treasury Bill interest rates were forced down to 0.01%. Yet, despite these massive inflationary measures, wholesale prices fell 9%, consumer prices fell 25%, and more people were unemployed in 1940 than in 1930.[37]

I think that in the past twelve months changes in velocity have become the dominant force in the economy again. They are counteracting changes in money supply, as they did then.

You'll remember, Chris, from my earlier letters about velocity that money responds to the law of supply and demand just as everything else does. If the supply of dollars rises, the value of each individual dollar falls and prices rise to compensate. That's inflation.

Inflation is not an increase in prices; it is an increase in the money supply that *causes* rising prices.

If the supply of dollars falls, the value of each individual dollar rises and prices fall. That's deflation.

---

36 THE ECONOMIST, February 20, 1999, p. 19.
37 All statistics from Historical Statistics of the U.S., CD-ROM, Cambridge University Press. Money supply is M1.

However, most analysts pay attention only to the supply of money; they forget the other equally important side of the coin—the demand for money.

If people do not *want* a particular type of currency, let's say the Mexican peso, then the value of a peso will fall; sellers will demand more pesos in trade for their goods or services. Prices in Mexico will rise even if there has been no change in the supply of pesos.

Also, if the demand for pesos rises, the value will rise and prices will fall even if there has been no change in the supply of pesos.

As I write this, the world is in a deflationary condition despite expanding money supplies because there is a big difference between deflation and a deflationary condition.

Changes in the demand for money can be so strong they can overwhelm changes in money supply.

This is what happened in the Great Depression. People were frightened and reluctant to spend their dollars. The government printed dollars rapidly, but not enough to offset this huge boost in the demand for money, and prices kept falling.

The newly printed dollars were not used in trade; they were stuffed into mattresses (that's a metaphor, they were commonly stuffed into safe deposit boxes) and so dollars were effectively removed from the economy.

In other words, in the Great Depression the speed at which the average dollar changed hands fell. This had the same effect as a fall in the money supply. In fact, it was so deflationary that it more than nullified the inflation of the money supply.

Velocity is the speed at which money changes hands. When the demand for money is high, velocity is low. When the demand for money is low, velocity is high.

A 10% decline in velocity has the same effect as a 10% decline in money supply.

For several years the Japanese have been so afraid of the future that they have been repeating the experience of the Great Depression. Japanese officials print a lot of yen, but the people won't spend it. The demand for money is so high, and velocity so low, that conditions remain deflationary.

Desperate to counteract the decline of velocity, Japanese officials have printed $6 billion worth of 1,000-yen coupons and handed them out free to shoppers. The coupons can be spent on anything. To make sure shoppers do not stuff them in mattresses, the coupons expire in six months.

It's not working. Six billion dollars has not been enough to counter Japan's drop in velocity.

As we watch the deflationary effects of falling velocity in Japan, we can see velocity running wild in the U.S. stock market. On average, all of Amazon.com's shares change hands twice each week.[38]

Velocity is never uniform, and I think the global economic crisis has caused it to become much less so. A few areas, like the Internet stocks, are raging hot while many others are freezing.

Chris, in another set of letters[39] I will give you a deeper understanding of money and velocity, but to help you better understand velocity now, I want to give you a quick overview. So, look at the cone illustration on the next page.

---

38 THE ECONOMIST, January 30, 1999, p.17.

39 Uncle Eric is referring to THE CLIPPER SHIP STRATEGY, an Uncle Eric book by Richard J. Maybury, published by Bluestocking Press, phone 800-959-8586, web site: www.BluestockingPress.com

When central banks inject money into the economy, the money does not go to everyone. Some get a lot, others get a little, and some get none.

The recipients of the money spend or invest it, usually in whatever happens to be fashionable.

So, the new money does not descend on the country in a uniform blanket. It goes into specific areas, like thick molasses poured from pitchers, filling a bathtub. Each dollar is one molecule of the fluid.

Imagine inverted cones of dollars. The bathtub is the general economy and the cones are the fashionable hot spots where the money is poured.

During the "Roaring 20s," for instance, stocks were fashionable. They became the cones, and we had the great stock market boom at the same time prices of consumer items and raw materials stayed flat or fell.

In cones where velocity is low, the fluid is thick and flows slowly. Each dollar changes hands slowly and so is not available to participate in as many transactions. Prices do not rise much.

In cones where velocity is high, the fluid is thin and flows quickly. Each dollar changes hands often, participating in many transactions, and drives prices up rapidly, as with the Internet stocks.

During the 1990s velocity was certainly high in Internet stocks and apparently low in raw materials. I think this will reverse in the new decade.

Each country has thousands of cones and each cone has a different temperature, a different velocity.

Chris, fear causes dramatic swings in velocity.

If people trust the currency, fear causes them to switch all their financial assets into cash, which they hoard. As a result, velocity plunges, having the same effect as a plunge in money supply.

If they don't trust the currency, people try to quickly swap it for goods, trusted foreign currencies, or precious metals. This has the same effect as a sudden and vast increase in money supply.

As I write this letter, Chris, U.S. and Iraqi forces have had some 70 shoot-outs since President Clinton bombed Iraq in December 1998 prior to his impeachment hearings.

The war between Eritrea and Ethiopia is worsening.

Normally quiet Uzbekistan has been hit by bombings and assassination attempts.

Indonesia's bloodshed is growing worse by the day.

Russia's chaos is spreading and hundreds of thousands of Russians have lost their savings in bank failures.

Kurds have rioted across Europe.

President Clinton has entered the war in Kosovo.

Chaos. Fear. Conditions globally are so confused that in Village A people might be hoarding cash, frightened of being without it, while in Village B down the road, they might be spending it wildly, afraid the cash will be inflated into worthlessness. Patchwork velocity; it varies from country to country, town to town, and day to day, depending on rumors.

On average, conditions seem deflationary right now, but there are exceptions—at least for a while—the principal one being the U.S. stock market.

For speculators, the trick to making big profits in this world of patchwork velocity is to be a buyer in cones you expect to get hot and a seller in those you expect to cool.

Nearly everyone who went to college since the Great Depression, including myself, was taught that the depression happened because central banks did not inflate enough. This is a terrible over-simplification, but it is what most still believe. So I think this time central bankers will go berserk printing money. The new decade will bring severe inflation, a repeat of the 1970s. Forewarned is forearmed. Study the 1970s. (To see what happened to investments, ask a librarian for THE WALL STREET JOURNALS from that decade.)

Chris, learn all you can about velocity and the demand for money. Their wide swings are likely to be the single most important force affecting your career, business, and investments for at least the next decade. Also study world events. Big changes are coming.

How you face the future, with fear or confidence, will depend on how much you understand and what you have done to protect yourself.

To help you get started, I'm sending you another set of letters that will help you understand what's happening in the Mideast and Europe.[40] Please get started on them immediately, Chris. Your future depends on understanding the past.

Uncle Eric

---

[40] Uncle Eric is referring to THE THOUSAND YEAR WAR IN THE MIDEAST: HOW IT AFFECTS YOU TODAY, an Uncle Eric book by Richard J. Maybury, published by Bluestocking Press, phone 800-959-8586, web site: www.BluestockingPress.com

18

A New, or Very Old, Form of Inflation

Dear Chris,

On the next page is an update of the Internet Stock Chart that appeared in my 1999 letter.

As you can see, prices changed, as I feared. Raw materials took off, rising 32%, while Internet stocks collapsed, falling 79%—wiping out many billions of dollars worth of savings of those who did not understand inflation and velocity. The following is my latest thinking on the subject of velocity.

After studying the government's behavior for more than three decades, I suspect we have been plunged into a new form of inflation. This form is well camouflaged—and possibly very dangerous. Let's cover some terminology, then some history.

When the government's spending exceeds its income, the shortfall is called the **federal deficit**. Each year's deficit is added to the total federal debt, or the "national" debt.

When someone loans money to the government they get an IOU. These IOUs are U.S. Treasury Bonds. Many of these bonds have been issued for ten years or longer, meaning lenders have given the government the use of their money for that long.

Officials also issue Treasury Notes and Treasury Bills, which are shorter-term bonds; some are for periods as short as three months.

The only important difference among them is their length; so, to keep things simple, I will refer to all of them as Treasury Bonds.

During the 1980s, federal officials began another of their wild borrowing sprees. In 1975, a $53 billion deficit had been considered frightening and grossly irresponsible. By 1992, the deficit for the month of February alone was $49 billion.

The federal debt that year was growing so fast it raised cries of alarm all over the world, and U.S. officials began to cut back their borrowing.

Then on September 11, 2001, the big "war on terrorism" began. Apparently reasoning that the war justified almost anything, the federal government returned to its old borrow-and-spend ways, adding $100 billion to its debt every few months.

In 1980, total federal debt, meaning total outstanding bonds, was $0.9 trillion, which was considered shocking.

By 1992, it was $3.8 trillion, and at the end of 2001, $6.2 trillion; as I write this in early 2004, it is $7.5 trillion.

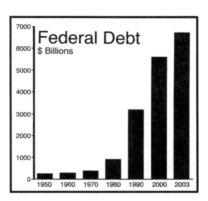

Chris, how much is $7.5 trillion? Here is a way to comprehend it.

Do you consider $1 million to be a lot of money? Imagine what you could buy with $1 million. Make a list. For instance, if that sports car you have written me about costs $40,000, a million dollars would enable you to buy 25 of them.

Now visualize $1 million in $100 bills laid end-to-end.

You would need 20 minutes to walk the length of this line of cash; it's about one mile.

Walk a line of $100 bills the length of the federal debt and it would take you 285 years.

If Columbus, when he stepped ashore in America, had immediately begun borrowing money at the rate of $10,000 per minute, by 2004 he would still not have borrowed the equivalent of today's federal debt.

Chris, something happened in the early 1980s. Apparently officials made a deliberate decision to borrow without limit, to wallpaper the world with their bonds.

Now let's go back further in history. Look at some of the paper money issued during the runaway inflation of the 1770s and 1780s.

The Connecticut bill says, "The possessor of this bill shall be paid by the treasurer of the State of Connecticut, ten shillings each, or other silver or gold coins equivalent, with interest at five percent per annum, by the 1st day of March, A.D. 1784. By order of Assembly. Dated at Hartford, the first day of June A.D. 1780."

On the eight-dollar bill issued by the government of Massachusetts in 1780 we find this promise: "The possessor of this bill shall be paid eight Spanish milled dollars by the thirty-first day of December, 1786, with interest in like money, at the rate of five per centum per annum.

The New Hampshire seven-dollar bill, Connecticut ten-shilling bill, and Rhode Island three-dollar bill were all issued in 1780, also paying five percent interest.

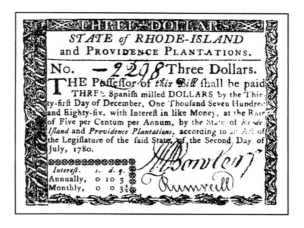

In modern English, the Rhode Island three-dollar bill says, "The possessor of this bill shall be paid three Spanish milled dollars[41] by the thirteenth day of December, One Thousand Seven Hundred and Eighty-six, with interest in like money, at the rate of five per centum per annum, by the State of Rhode Island and Providence Plantations, according to an act of the legislature of the said state, of the second day of July 1780."

---

[41] A Spanish milled dollar (or "piece of eight") was the most commonly circulated money in the American colonies. It was about 27 grams (slightly less than one ounce) of silver.

Chris, why would a government pay interest on its currency?

It is because people were afraid to accept depreciating paper money in trade for their goods and services. Governments had to offer an extra reward to induce them to take the risk.

Suppose you had been around in those days and had a mattress stuffed with paper money, some of which paid interest and some of which didn't. Which bills would you have spent and which would you have saved?

You'd have saved the ones paying interest, right?

So, which bills would have had higher money demand and lower "velocity" of circulation?

The ones paying interest.

Money that is in lower demand will circulate faster and affect prices the same way as an increase in the money supply. Money in greater demand will circulate slower and have the same effect as a decrease in the money supply.

Here is my key point, Chris: A government can print more interest-bearing money than non-interest bearing money because interest-bearing money does not affect prices as much. Money stuffed in a mattress is effectively withdrawn from the economy.

Now, here's my theory about what government officials have been doing to us in recent decades.

During the monetary crisis in 1979-80, demand for paper money plunged and soaring demand for precious metals drove gold to $850 per ounce and silver to $50 per ounce. Officials were in emergency meetings trying to figure out what to do. If they continued inflating as much as they wanted to, they might tip the entire world into the biggest hyperinflation ever known.

I think they hit on the idea of copying the practice of 200 years earlier. Federal officials now regard their bonds not as debt because they intend never to repay it (how could anyone repay a $7.5 trillion debt?) but as low-velocity cash they can print and spend without limit.

They can print a lot more of this cash because it does not circulate like the greenbacks in our wallets — so it has much less effect on prices.

While the velocity of a $1 Federal Reserve Note (FRN — one of those "dollars" in your wallet) is probably 100 or more, the velocity of a 30-year Treasury Bond might be less than 1, meaning it might change hands less than once per year.

This means a $10,000 bond would have less than a hundredth the impact on prices as $10,000 in FRNs.

Assuming officials did decide to go this route in 1980, their thinking would be easy to see: We haven't a prayer of ever repaying a trillion dollars in debt, so if we are going to default on a trillion, why not five trillion? Or fifty trillion? Or nine-hundred gazillion? And, when interest payments become unmanageable, we'll print bonds to pay those, too.

The same reasoning as in 1780.

The mechanics of the plan would be simple. To boost their spending, they'd print bonds, then trade the bonds for FRNs, and spend the FRNs. The FRNs would continue to circulate, but the bonds would not, at least not much, so the supply of bonds could be increased almost without limit.

A brilliant scheme.

Or, I should say, brilliant until bond holders figure out what is happening and stop accepting the government's bonds.

Another way to look at the scheme is that officials are trading their new low-velocity money (bonds) for old high-velocity money (FRNs). Since 1980, the Treasury Bond money supply has been increased a whopping $6.6 trillion, but this $6.6 trillion has little velocity and little effect on prices.

So far.

What happens, Chris, when the world begins to understand the scheme and realizes federal officials plan to print bonds until every person on earth has a wheelbarrow full?

What happened in 1979 when they began to understand the government's plan to print unlimited amounts of FRNs?

My guess is that overnight these trillions of dollars worth of bonds will be thrown into the investment markets by people wanting to get rid of them. The bonds will be traded for FRNs, which will be immediately traded for real estate, precious metals, or anything else with value that is not tied rigidly to the value of paper dollars.

In other words, Chris, overnight this entire $7.5 trillion of low-velocity cash will become high-velocity cash. In effect, the present official $1.3 trillion money supply[42] will be instantly inflated to $8.8 trillion.

Chris, does this make the hair on the back of your neck stand up? It should.

The public outcry over the federal debt in the early 1990s looked like the beginning of the backlash—the unraveling of the bond scheme. But officials apparently got scared and slowed their borrowing enough to quiet things down. After a few years the emergency had passed, and the debt was no longer seen as a threat.

It looks to me that by the time 9-11 came along officials felt safe in returning to deficit spending, meaning a revival of the bond scheme.

---

[42] Using the M1 measure of money supply.

Chris, how long will it be until investors begin to get afraid of holding U.S. bonds?

Predicting human behavior is always a high-risk game. Humans have free wills and they change their minds continually; so we cannot know when they will begin to flee bonds.

But, here is a signal we can watch. It is called the yield curve.

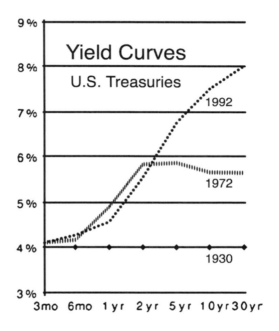

The yield curve is an illustration of the difference between interest paid on short-term bonds and long-term bonds.

In March of 1992, for instance, 3-month Treasury Bonds were paying about 4%, two-year Treasury Bonds were paying about 6%, and 30-year Treasuries around 8%. I have plotted these rates on the chart so you can see the curve.

A large difference between short-term and long-term bonds means investors are nervous about owning long-term bonds. They don't like the risk that inflation will wipe out the value of the money before the IOUs are paid off.

In other words, they do not like the fact that they might loan out dollars each worth one loaf of bread and years later get back dollars worth only one slice. They demand higher interest rates as compensation for taking this risk.

For a 3-month bond, the risk is much lower because the money is returned in just 90 days; so the interest rate is lower.

Look at the chart again, Chris. Before the 1930s, the dollar was convertible to gold and yield curves were flat. A 30-year bond earned the same interest as a 3-month bond because investors were confident the value of the money would not decline.

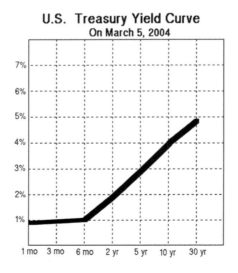

U.S. Treasury Yield Curve
On March 5, 2004

By 1992, the yield curve was far steeper than in the days of the gold standard. This is persuasive evidence that investors were becoming afraid to hold bonds.

Chris, I researched back to the year 1900 and could not find any other time when the yield curve of U.S. bonds was as steep as in the 1990s. This is probably why U.S. officials got scared and slowed their borrowing. They were afraid the yield curve was telling them that a disaster—a flight from their bonds—was just around the corner.

But when the war came along, caution was apparently thrown to the wind.

Watch the yield curve, Chris, it is published daily in THE WALL STREET JOURNAL. The steeper it becomes, I think, the closer we are to the big panic.

As for that often-asked question—will we have a hyperinflation or depression?—the answer is that we are already in a hyperinflation. The $7.5 trillion in bonds is a huge paper money overhang poised to avalanche into the economy the moment investors become afraid to hold the bonds. Most newly created money is being diverted into this overhang where it isn't having much affect on prices—yet. I suspect that instead of a gradual increase in prices over several years, we will get it all in a single week or month when this overhang breaks loose.

A key question now is: how many more trillions in U.S. bonds can the world absorb? Whatever that number is, the day we reach it will be most interesting.

In the meantime, Chris, when someone tells you history is useless and a waste of time, you might point to the interest-bearing money issued during the American Revolution, then to today's federal debt, and ask: so you think history does not repeat?

Uncle Eric

Inflation is like sin; every government denounces it and every government practices it.

—Sir Frederick Keith-Ross (1887-1968)
quoted in THE OBSERVER, June 30, 1957

The issuers may have, and in the case of government paper, always have, a direct interest in lowering the value of the currency, because it is the medium in which their own debts are computed.

—John Stuart Mill, (1806-1873)
Principles of Political Economy, ed. Ashley
Bk.III, Ch. XIII,1, p.544

Bibliography

- FIAT MONEY INFLATION IN FRANCE by Andrew Dickson White, Foundation for Economic Education, Irvington-on-Hudson, NY.

- THE GREAT INFLATION by William Guttmann and Patricia Meehan, Gordon & Cremonesi, Great Britain, 1975, ISBN 0-86033-035-4.

- EXTRAORDINARY POPULAR DELUSIONS AND THE MADNESS OF CROWDS by Charles Mackay, LL.D., Harmony Books, NY.

Book Suppliers

- ° Advocates for Self-Government, Inc., phone: 800-932-1776, web site: www.self-gov.org

- ° Bluestocking Press, phone: 800-959-8586, web site: www.BluestockingPress.com

- ° Foundation for Economic Education, phone: 800-960-4FEE, web site: www.fee.org

- ° Liberty Tree Network, phone: 800-927-8733, web site: www.liberty-tree.org

**Contact your librarian or a used bookstore
for locating out-of-print books**.

Glossary

ANOMALY. A strange exception to what would be expected.

ASSIGNAT. French paper money.

BLACK MARKET. The production, sale, or trade of goods or services against the wishes of the government. Example: Liquor was a black market product during the "Prohibition Era."

BLIND-SIDED. A football term meaning to be hit from one direction while looking in the other direction.

BOND. An IOU. Bond usually means a long-term IOU— several years or decades, not months.

BUSINESS CYCLE. The boom/bust cycle. Prosperity followed by recession followed by prosperity followed by recession, and so forth.

CONSUMER PRICE INDEX. The U.S. Government's estimate of the overall price level of goods purchased by consumers.

COUP D' ETAT. Violent overthrow of the government by a small group of individuals.

DEFLATION. Commonly used to mean a decrease in prices. Actually a decrease in the amount of money, which causes a decrease in prices. Also usually causes depressions and falling prices.

DEMAND FOR MONEY. The desire to hold money rather than trade it away. High demand for money means money is traded away reluctantly. Low demand for money means money is traded away quickly.

DEPRESSION. The correction period following an inflation. Usually includes a lot of business failures and unemployment.

DICTATOR. Someone who rules with absolute, arbitrary power and control.

DOUBLE-DIGIT INFLATION. Price increases rising at 10 to 99 percent per year due to inflation.

ECONOMICS. The study of the production and distribution of wealth (goods and services).

FED. See Federal Reserve.

FEDERAL DEFICIT. The shortfall that results when the government's spending exceeds its income. Each year's deficit is added to the total federal debt, or the "national" debt.

FEDERAL RESERVE. The central bank of the U.S. Controls the supply of money and attempts to control interest rates.

FIAT. Something easily done or undone at the whim of authorities. Whimsical.

FIAT LAW. Law not logically derived from ethical principles. Law made up by lawmakers according to the rule: whatever appears necessary.

FIAT MONEY. Money created by a legal tender law. Money not backed by gold or silver.

FIRST STAGE INFLATION. In the first stage, prices do not rise as fast as the money supply does because people don't understand what is happening. Some delay their spending in hopes prices will fall back. In effect, they take some of the money out of circulation as the government is pumping it in. This was France in 1790.

FORECAST. Predict.

FREEZE. To hold in place. In economics, "freeze" is usually used in reference to prices or supplies of goods. A government can forbid traders to change their prices or forbid them to sell or transport their goods.

GNP. See Gross National Product.

GRAIN EMBARGO. A law forbidding farmers to sell grain to certain buyers.

GROSS NATIONAL PRODUCT. The government's estimate of the production of finished goods and services.

HOT MONEY. Money changing hands quickly.

HYPERINFLATION. An inflation in which prices are rising at triple-digit (or more) rates per year.

ILLIQUID. Not easily sold or traded. Real estate is illiquid compared to stocks, for instance.

INFLATION. Commonly used to mean an increase in prices. Actually an increase in the amount of money that causes an increase in prices by reducing the value of each unit of money.

INJECTION EFFECT. The changes that occur on Wall Street (the financial world) and Main Street (where most of us live and work) when the government injects new money into the economy.

INTEREST. The price of renting money. When the supply of money is less than the demand, the interest rates rise.

LEGAL TENDER LAW. A law saying you will be punished if you do not accept a given type of money in trade for your goods or services.

LIQUID. Easily sold or traded.

MANDAT. The French paper money that replaced the assignat.

MONEY. The most easily traded thing in a society. Economists call it the most liquid commodity.

MONEY SUPPLY. The amount of money in a country or economy. In recent years economists have begun to try to measure the total world money supply as well as the money supplies of individual countries.

PAPER MONEY. Today usually means fiat money. Money created by legal tender laws.

POLITICAL POWER. The privilege of using force on persons who have not harmed anyone. The legal privilege of backing one's decisions with violence or threats of violence. Not the same thing as influence, which implies that a person has the option to walk away.

RUN. A sudden strong surge of buying or selling. Also, a panic, usually either by depositors to remove their money from a bank, or by holders of a currency or investment to quickly trade the currency or investment away. A "run on the dollar" would mean holders of dollars were in a panic to trade their dollars for something they value or trust more.

RUNAWAY INFLATION. A hyperinflation. Prices rising rapidly.

SECOND STAGE INFLATION. In the second stage, many people have begun to understand what is happening and are spending their money quickly. Prices rise faster than the money supply because each unit of the money is changing hands fast, making more transactions possible. Wanting to get rid of it fast, many are willing to accept less for it.

SOVIET BLOC. The Soviet Bloc was the Soviet Empire — the Soviet Union plus the nations it controlled. This was a huge area, about one-sixth of all the land on earth.

SOVIET UNION. The Soviet government was a long-time enemy of the U.S. Government. The Soviet Union was made up of these countries: Russia, Estonia, Latvia, Lithuania, Belarus, Ukraine, Moldova, Georgia, Armenia, Azerbaijan, Kazakhstan, Uzbekistan, Turkmenistan, Tajikistan, and Kirgizstan.

THIRD STAGE INFLATION. In the third stage (the runaway) the whole population is in a panic to get rid of the money as soon as they get their hands on it, and the money declines to its real value, which is the value of scrap paper.

VELOCITY. The speed at which money changes hands. A measure of the demand for money.

About Richard J. Maybury

Richard Maybury, also known as Uncle Eric, is a world renowned author, lecturer and geopolitical analyst. He consults with business firms in the U.S. and Europe. Richard is the former Global Affairs editor of MONEYWORLD and widely regarded as one of the finest free-market writers in America. Mr. Maybury's articles have appeared in THE WALL STREET JOURNAL, USA TODAY, and other major publications.

Richard Maybury has penned eleven books in the Uncle Eric series. His books have been endorsed by top business leaders including former U.S. Treasury Secretary William Simon, and he has been interviewed on more than 250 radio and TV shows across America.

He has been married for more than 35 years, has lived abroad, traveled around the world, and visited 48 states and 40 countries.

He is truly a teacher for all ages.

Index

"You probably want to make money. There's nothing wrong with that. In fact, there's a lot that is very good about it. It means that you are willing to do things that other people will pay for. It helps you. It helps them.

"Even if making money isn't your main goal, remember that money is the way we keep accounts these days. If you don't have any money, things will be harder for you than if you have some. Some people don't need much to let them do what they want. Some people need a lot. And it all has to come from some place. Friends can give it to you. Your parents can give it to you. But someone has to have earned it sometime, someway, someplace.

"Above everything else, you want to earn one thing that is even more important than money. You want to earn self-esteem. You want to feel good about yourself. You want to be able to look anyone in the world straight in their eyes and gain their respect. You want to respect yourself.

"Money is a way to keep track of how well you're doing. It's just one way. The way you feel about yourself is the bottom line. You should be able to make money and lose money without ever losing your own sense of self-worth and self-respect. Remember, the object is for you to make money by doing useful things, things that other people will voluntarily pay for. You make the money. The money doesn't make you!"

—Karl Hess, CAPITALISM FOR KIDS
published by Bluestocking Press

Bluestocking Press

Bluestocking Press publishes the following:

1) Richard J. Maybury's Uncle Eric books (and the accompanying student study guides for the Uncle Eric books)

2) Karl Hess' CAPITALISM FOR KIDS

3) Kathryn Daniels' COMMON SENSE BUSINESS FOR KIDS

4) ECONOMICS: A FREE MARKET READER

5) LAURA INGALLS WILDER AND ROSE WILDER LANE HISTORICAL TIMETABLE

Visit the BLUESTOCKING PRESS CATALOG online at
www.BluestockingPress.com

To order by phone, contact Bluestocking Press
(See contact information
on the last page of this book.)

Published by Bluestocking Press

Uncle Eric Books by Richard J. Maybury

UNCLE ERIC TALKS ABOUT PERSONAL, CAREER, AND FINANCIAL SECURITY

WHATEVER HAPPENED TO PENNY CANDY?

WHATEVER HAPPENED TO JUSTICE?

ARE YOU LIBERAL? CONSERVATIVE? OR CONFUSED?

ANCIENT ROME: HOW IT AFFECTS YOU TODAY

EVALUATING BOOKS: WHAT WOULD THOMAS JEFFERSON THINK ABOUT THIS?

THE MONEY MYSTERY

THE CLIPPER SHIP STRATEGY

THE THOUSAND YEAR WAR IN THE MIDEAST

WORLD WAR I: THE REST OF THE STORY

WORLD WAR II: THE REST OF THE STORY

Bluestocking Guides (study guides for the Uncle Eric books)
by Jane A. Williams and/or Kathryn Daniels

Each Study Guide includes some or all of the following:

1) chapter-by-chapter comprehension questions and answers

2) application questions and answers

3) research activities

4) essay assignments

5) thought questions

6) final exam

More Bluestocking Press Titles

LAURA INGALLS WILDER AND ROSE WILDER LANE HISTORICAL TIMETABLE

CAPITALISM FOR KIDS: GROWING UP TO BE YOUR OWN BOSS by Karl Hess

COMMON SENSE BUSINESS FOR KIDS by Kathryn Daniels

ECONOMICS: A FREE MARKET READER edited by Jane Williams & Kathryn Daniels

Order information: Order any of the above by phone or online from:

Bluestocking Press
Phone: 800-959-8586

email: CustomerService@BluestockingPress.com

web site: www.BluestockingPress.com